The Little Book of Maths from Stories

Using story books to support mathematical learning

Inspired by
Neil Griffiths

Edited by Sally Featherstone

Illustrations by Martha Hardy

Little Books with **BIG** ideas®

The Little Book of Maths from Stories

ISBN 1 905019 25 4

© Featherstone Education Ltd, 2005
Text © Neil Griffiths, Sally Featherstone, 2005
Series Editor, Sally Featherstone

First published in the UK, May 2005

'Little Books' is a trade mark of Featherstone Education Ltd

Published in the United Kingdom by
Featherstone Education Ltd
44 - 46 High Street
Husbands Bosworth
Leicestershire
LE17 6LP

Printed in the UK on paper produced in the European Union from managed, sustainable forests

Contents

Introduction

The aim of this Little Book is to provide practitioners with ideas for developing mathematics using high quality picture books and well known rhymes. The book is intended for practitioners working with young children in early years settings and, of course, at home.

The National Numeracy Strategy (1999) indicated that:

> "....stories, rhymes and songs can be chosen which rely for their appeal on the pleasure of counting, the sequencing of events and use of everyday words to describe position or direction."

For mathematics to be relevant to the children, it should be applied to particular and familiar situations, allowing children to be able to recognise when to use and practise it. Young children therefore need to be given meaningful, interesting, practical activities which stimulate them and encourage them to want to learn.

> "Mathematical Activities for young children must be set within the experience of everyday life and must involve them in active exploration of the world around them"
>
> Planning for Progression
> Inspection and Advisory Services, Wales.

Children often relate closely to books, their characters, experiences and story lines, and familiar stories can therefore often help children to relate to the world around them. It therefore seems a logical extension to use them as a source of activities and games to develop mathematical learning.

Using stories and rhymes for mathematics will give:

- ☺ A context for learning
- ☺ Relevance
- ☺ A clear purpose
- ☺ Practical application
- ☺ Visual reinforcement
- ☺ Stimulus for wanting to learn
- ☺ Engagement and fun!

This book is intended to help you to provide and structure a range of exciting mathematical activities and investigations using stories and rhymes as a starting point for exploration. Most activities use resources that can be easily found or are readily available in an early years setting.

Each section will offer a different approach for using picture books, indicating:

'What to do'
'What you need'
'Key vocabulary'
'Further activities'
and 'Key learning goals in mathematics'.

In addition to addressing all the learning goals for mathematics at both the Foundation Stage and early stages of the National Curriculum at KS1, each story will also offer opportunities for activities in other areas of the curriculum.

Communication and language skills are key to all areas of learning; Personal and social development benefits when children are involved in enjoyable activities. Stories add examples of Knowledge and Understanding of the World. Physical and creative development are central to activities in all early years settings.

Additional Early Learning Goals

You will find mathematical goals on each activity page. Some of the additional goals addressed are listed here:

Personal, Social and Emotional Development

- continue to be excited and motivated to learn;
- be confident to try new activities, initiate ideas and speak in a familiar group;
- maintain attention, concentration and sit quietly when appropriate;
- respond to significant experiences, sharing a range of feelings when appropriate;
- form good relationships;
- work as part of a group or class.

Communication, language and literacy

- enjoy listening to and using spoken and written language;
- sustain attentive listening;
- listen with enjoyment and respond to stories;
- extend their vocabulary;
- speak clearly;
- use language to imagine and recreate roles;
- use talk to organise, sequence and clarify ideas;
- show an understanding of the elements of stories.

Knowledge and Understanding of the World

- investigate objects and materials by using all their senses as appropriate;
- look clearly at similarities, differences, pattern and change;
- ask questions about why things happen.

Physical Development

- move with confidence, imagination and safety;
- travel around, under, over and through equipment;
- show awareness of space;
- use a range of small equipment.

Creative Development

- explore colour, texture, shape, form and space in two and three dimensions;
- sing simple songs;
- use their imagination in role play.

Getting Started

Planning and preparation

Foundation Stage practitioners and teachers in Key Stage 1 have always valued the contribution that high quality picture books can offer to their work and to the experiences of children. Books are a staple of the early years diet and are used daily to reinforce and extend language learning.

Some stories have a declared mathematical intention. They involve counting, shape, pattern etc. and in this way are 'easier' to use for maths sessions. However, these books and many others can be used in inventive ways to develop mathematical themes loosely or closely linked to the aspects of the Curriculum for Maths in the Foundation Stage and Key Stage 1.

Time is well spent in taking a new look at the books in your collection with a 'mathematical eye', looking for opportunities for the following mathematical skills and concepts. Ask yourself if the story has potential for exploring:

? shape, size, and relationships between them;

? colour, pattern, line;

? counting and numbers (on, back, twos, threes);

? sequences and journeys (stories are sequences of events, and sequencing is a key maths concept);

? sorting, grouping;

? calculating (more, less, sharing, multiplying);

? detail in illustration, encouraging children to look for similarities, differences, repeated events and objects;

? rhyme, rhythm and sound patterns (these all help counting);

? solving problems and challenges;

? using maths in real life;

? maths out of doors.

You may also want to start a collection of your own or bought Story Sacks with mathematical themes.

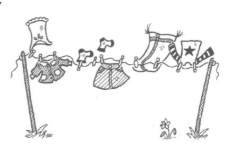

Mathematical story sessions

When you see a professional story teller working with a group of children, the process looks so easy! Remember that professionals spend a lot of time preparing for their sessions, they have experience of the way things go, the best stories to use, the sort of questions children ask and comments they make.

You need to be just as well prepared for your story sessions, then they will be successful, enjoyable and profitable experiences for you and for the children. Some tips:

*   Always read the story before telling it to a group of children. Experienced practitioners can get away with impromptu story telling some times, but the story sessions described in the book have key mathematical intentions, and you need to be familiar with the book in order to achieve these intentions and not be distracted or surprised by the story.

*   Prepare your resources in advance and have them handy, so you don't have to break off to collect a pen or look for a particular animal. If the session involves making props such as masks or headbands, have the equipment to hand in a basket or box.

*   Think about your particular group of children when preparing a story. Different groups may need a story simplifying or an extension to an activity. Think about their age and stage of development.

*   Don't make the session too long; a short enjoyable story time will be far more effective than a long one where children 'switch off' or lose their interest and enthusiasm.

The Little Book of Maths from Stories

* Make sure everyone can see the pictures in the book clearly. It's unrealistic to expect children to concentrate on something, join in discussion and answer questions if they don't feel part of the action.
* Check the group size. It's better to have two smaller sessions than one big group if you can. Smaller groups mean everyone can contribute and join in the activities, or take part in playing out the story.
* Select your venue! Sometimes it's easier to work round a table, sometimes to sit on a carpet or cushions. Sometimes you may want to be outside, other times in the role play area, the writing area, the quiet corner or the hall. Think flexibly and match your venue to the activity.
* Remember to leave the book somewhere obvious for children to return to later. You could have a special place, book stand or table with props for the 'Book of the Day' or 'Book of the Week'. Remember, if you are using a story or other book for mathematical activities, you should leave it in your maths area, not the book corner!

And finally, **enjoy the book and read it all the way through before starting mathematical activities. Read with as much expression as you can, use character voices, puppets or props to help you. You could even dress up or sit on a special story chair.**

Get the children used to looking and listening to the uninterrupted story before discussion and questions.

Ten in a Bed
Using illustrations

This simple story book has great illustrations, as well as opportunities for counting on and back. Part of becoming a mathematician is becoming a good observer. Ten in a Bed has plenty of opportunities to spot things and to look at the importance of illustrations and how they help the story. Other stories with plenty to talk about are: Pass the Parcel; My Mum and Dad Make me Laugh; The Very Hungry Caterpillar; The Tiger who came to Tea; Bear in a Square; Pants; Shapes.

What you need:

☆ a range of books with interesting illustrations.
Take account of the age of the children when looking at complexity and detail. Also remember that any close observation activity is much better done in small groups.

Some Key Vocabulary:

long	over	straight
shape	in front	below
solid	tall	beside
under	curved	high
bottom	shapes	round
longest	above	top
pattern	next to	
corner	short	

We are fortunate in this country to have the most wonderful collection of high quality picture books available in bookshops and libraries. These books contain outstanding illustrations that are colourful and eye-catching, providing excellent starting points for discussion and questions.

Good illustrations are often full of **examples of shape, pattern, size and use of space**. Be selective and make a collection of books with quality illustrations to support mathematical concepts. **Ask your librarian or local children's bookshop for suggestions**. Read reviews in magazines and on the Internet.

What you do:

1. If you are working on close observation of pictures, always check that all children in the group can see. Adjust the group size to the size of the book!

2. Always read the book through first from start to finish, allowing the children to enjoy the story and the illustrations.

3. Encourage free discussion and careful observation of individual pages and illustrations.

4. Try to focus on mathematical discussion and activities such as counting, spotting differences and similarities, colour, shape, distance and pattern.

5. For younger children choose illustrations that are simple and uncluttered.

6. For more able children you could use more intricate illustration styles.

And another idea . . .

* Cut up some books to provide single illustrations for obser-vation, counting, shape etc.
* Explore wrapping paper designs together. They provide excellent opportunities for discussion.

Links with the Early Learning Goals

MD use language such as 'greater', 'smaller' to compare quantities;
talk about simple patterns;
use language such as 'circle' or 'bigger';
use everyday words to describe position.

Two Little Eyes

Using songs and rhymes

There are hundreds of number songs and rhymes - Two Little Eyes has a mixture of well known and new rhymes to help counting and maths vocabulary at home as well as at school. You might want to buy more than one copy and add it to your 'home lending' library. This Little Puffin contains lots of counting rhymes.

What you need:

☆ just the book, somewhere to sit and some children!

Some Key Vocabulary:

hands	1-5	fat
fingers	count	thin
arms	more	short
mouth	less	tall
eyes	big	under
ears	middle	over
feet	size	
numbers	small	

Spend a few minutes every day singing or saying number songs and rhymes. Time spent doing this will not be wasted, and children will collect a selection of their favourites. Encourage parents to sing and say the rhymes and songs at home by providing 'take home' lists, sheets or little books illustrated with photos or children's pictures.

What you do:

1. Collect together a group of children. If you know the rhymes off by heart it will be easier to manage the session, particularly with a larger group.
2. Keep the pace snappy and don't go on too long - little and often will be best, and you can use these activities in spare minutes between other activities or while waiting for other children to clear up, join the group, finish another activity.
3. Don't stop to discuss the number aspects, just keep the activity going. You can explore their understanding of the vocabulary and other concepts in other group times.
4. Encourage everyone in your team to use these minutes for counting and number activities and you will be surprised at the difference it makes to children's mathematical learning, as well as being fun for everyone.
5. Let children choose the rhymes and songs and lead the action in the group, but don't force them if they are uncertain or anxious.
6. Add songs and rhymes in community and other languages.

And another idea . . .

* Make up some counting rhymes of your own using familiar tunes.
* Record the songs and rhymes for children to play back themselves.

Links with the Early Learning Goals

MD use mathematical language;
   say and use numbers from 1 to 10;
CD sing simple songs;
CLL enjoy songs and rhymes.

Goldilocks

Using traditional stories

Goldilocks and other traditional tales give great opportunities for learning counting, sorting, matching and other maths vocabulary. This one is particularly helpful for learning about size and one-to-one correspondence, essential for accurate counting and matching. Try telling the story without the book, so you have both hands free for the props!

What you need:

☆ the Three Bears story (in a book or in your head!)
☆ three different sized bears
☆ three bowls, spoons (and possibly chairs and beds)
☆ a doll to be Goldilocks

Some Key Vocabulary:

bear	bowl	downstairs
father	spoon	along
mother	bed	through
baby	chair	next
big	one	after
middle	two	
small	three	
size	upstairs	

Having some props, puppets or characters really helps children to engage with the story and the concepts you are focusing on. Dramatising a story also helps children to understand concepts such as size and order, by experiencing them with their whole bodies.

What you do:

1. Read or tell the story, using the props to help with visualisation. Go straight through, don't stop for questions or explanations. You could get the children to help with this.
2. Tell the story again, stopping to ask questions (remember this is a maths experience). Focus on:
   size (small, bigger, biggest; big, smaller, smallest)
   matching (eg Which spoon goes with this bowl?)
   shape (try looking for shapes in the story; curves, circles, squares) sequence (what happened before, next, after that).
3. Sing 'When Goldilocks went to the House of the Bears', encouraging the children to use their fingers to count 'One, two, three.'
4. Dramatise the story by being big, medium and small bears, holding big, medium and small bowls, eating from big, medium and small spoons, sitting on big, medium and small chairs or beds.
   Or dramatise the story in episodes to reinforce sequence and order.

And another idea . . .

* Make your role play corner into The Three Bears' house and play the story again.
* Use recycled materials to make different sized beds and chairs for your teddies.

Links with the Early Learning Goals

MD say and use number names in order in familiar contexts;
count reliably up to 10 everyday objects;
use language such as circle, or bigger to describe the shape and size of solids and flat shapes.

Someone Bigger

Mathematical language

A story about a boy, his dad, a kite and a windy day gives many openings for using and understanding mathematical language. It also has a clear message that bigger is not necessarily better! It would be a good addition to a collection of stories with mathematical language.

Stories are a useful way of introducing vocabulary in the context of an exciting story line.

What you need:

☆ the book 'Someone Bigger'
☆ a kite with a long string
☆ small world people and animals to attach to the kite string (or you could use card figures and animals instead)

Some Key Vocabulary:

bigger	second	light
smaller	third	longer
older	fourth	shorter
younger	fifth etc.	high
next	up	higher
after	down	
first	heavy	

The Little Book of Maths from Stories

Early years practitioners are very good at making the most of stories to help children with language concepts. It is also important that young mathematicians learn the **language and vocabulary of maths** as soon as possible. Your skill as a practitioner is in **spotting opportunities** to include mathematical vocabulary thinking and language wherever you can.

What you do:

1. Use your own experience and the knowledge of colleagues, librarians and others to make a good collection of books rich in mathematical vocabulary and concepts.
2. Read the story through without pausing.
3. Now read the story again, pausing to check that the children understand the vocabulary.
4. Begin to ask questions about what happens next, who is next to hang on the string, who is first, second etc.
5. Talk about bigger, stronger, older, younger, smaller.
6. Explore how the first person on the kite string is the last person to land at the end of the story.
7. Discuss how you could tie the people and animals on the string in the story order, and then untie them again. Use the language of ordinal numbers - first, second, third, last etc.
8. Get the children to stand in a line and be the characters in the story. Talk about first, second etc.
9. Use the toy kite to help you play out the story.

And another idea . . .

* Make some kites and decorate them with numbers, shapes and patterns.
* Play ordinals games in small groups: 'First person stand up,' 'Third person wave,' etc.

Links with the Early Learning Goals

MD   use everyday words to describe position; say and use number names in order in familiar contexts; use language such as greater, smaller, heavier or lighter.

Ten in a Bed
A counting story

A vast number of picture books can now be collected to encourage and include counting in stories. Remember the power of high quality illustrations, simple repetitive text and rhyme as a motor for memory. 'Ten in a Bed' has great illustrations, and it is also a great story for practising counting on and back.

What you need:
- ☆ the book
- ☆ some soft toys
- ☆ a blanket or doll's bed
- ☆ a doll (or a real child)

Some Key Vocabulary:

numbers	out/in	beside
1- 10	back	behind
more/less	up	on top
one more	down	together
one less	under	
count	over	

The stories in this section have a focus on 'Number as labels and for counting'. The books can also be used for other mathematical activities and conversations, and of course, close observation, sequencing, anticipation, problem solving and mathematical vocabulary run through-out all sessions.

What you do:

1. Read the story together.
2. Now do some picture spotting and language work using the vocabulary of position and size.
3. Read it again, using the soft toys or involving a child. Let the children help you remove and then add the toys in the right order.
4. As you retell the story, get the children involved by holding up the number of fingers for the toys in the bed and the toys out of the bed. This story is great for exploring the following number concepts (depending on the age and mathematical level of the group):
   ☆ counting
   ☆ one more
   ☆ one less
   ☆ ordering and ordinal numbers (first, second etc)
   ☆ combining sets (looking at and counting the number of toys in the bed and out of the bed on each page)
   ☆ older children could use the story to explore number bonds to 10!

And another idea . . .

* Sing 'Ten Green Bottles' and 'Ten in the Bed'.
* Make some number labels from 1-10 and add them to a row (or bed) full of toys or children.

Links with the Early Learning Goals

MD use everyday words to describe position;
say and use number names in order in familiar contexts;
use language such as greater, smaller, heavier or lighter.

Balloon
Remembering & following sequences

A story is a narrative recounting a sequence or series of events. Sequencing is a skill in both literacy and numeracy, and stories can provide wonderful opportunities to involve children in sequencing activities. Balloon is a story with a strong story line and plenty of opportunities for pausing to recap, to predict and to use sequential language within a simple and familiar story line. You can just use the story for a sequencing session or you could turn 2 copies into a sequencing game for use again and again.

What you need:

☆ 2 copies of the book to make the sequencing cards
☆ laminating facilities or plastic envelopes if you want the cards to last!
☆ a washing line and pegs

Some Key Vocabulary:

first	next to	place
second	after	last
third	left	next
beginning	right	between
end	order	
middle	beside	
before	sequence	

What you do:

1. Make the sequencing cards. You may like to involve the children in this, in which case you can read the story with them first to help familiarise them with the sequence of the story.
2. Cut the books into separate pages.
3. For younger children to use, you could cut the words off so they can concentrate on the pictures. For older children, the text will provide additional cues to help with the sequence.
4. Cover the picture on the back of each page with white paper (so the children are not confused!).
5. Cover the page numbers (you could use correction fluid).
6. Now start with two pictures. Ask 'Which comes first in the story?' 'Which comes last?' Encourage the children to talk about their decisions and give reasons for their choices. Peg their suggestions on the washing line or put them on the carpet or table.
7. Add two more pictures and discuss where they go. Add them to your sequence. Don't always give children the VERY next picture, this will stimulate discussion and reorganisation of the pictures.
8. As you add more cards, tell the story sequence so far. It always helps children to talk through the sequence and point to each picture as they do.
9. As the children work on the sequence, keep asking them to justify their choices and encourage them to try telling the story to check.

And another idea . . .

* Sequence props for a story.
* Make bead sequences on laces.
* Put a line of objects on a table, look hard at them together, cover and try to remember the order.

Links with the Early Learning Goals

MD use everyday words to describe position; use developing mathematical ideas and methods to solve practical problems; use language such as greater, smaller, heavier or lighter to compare quantities.

The Very Hungry Caterpillar

The language of sequences

The Very Hungry Caterpillar is a long-standing favourite of children and practitioners. It also offers more challenging opportunities for sequencing, memory and anticipation which build on those in Balloon. You could make books into sequencing cards, but there are many more sequencing activities to do with this story!

What you need:

☆ the book
☆ fruit and other food for counting (plastic, pictures or real)
☆ some simple puppets for the caterpillar, pupa and butterfly

Some key vocabulary

Monday	up/on	fat
Tuesday	out	small
Wednesday	little	around
Thursday	tiny	inside
Friday	through	grow
Saturday	night	numbers
Sunday	big	1-9

This book can also be used for many **other mathematical activities**;
length, weight, size, growth, transformation
counting, one more, one less, addition, pattern
2D shape, symmetry, position
sorting and matching, counting on, ordinal numbers

What you do:

1. Collect the props and the story. You could make some simple finger puppet caterpillars from glove fingers or felt, so everyone can join in, or have enough food props for everyone to have one.
2. Read the story right through first.
3. Now start again and read the story with your chosen props.
4. Pause to talk about what comes next. You could:
    * pause before turning a page to ask 'What happens now?'
    * put the food props out and let children select what comes next;
    * talk about the sequence of the life of the caterpillar from egg to butterfly;
    * let the children dress in simple masks or pieces of fabric to play out the sequence of the story;
    * dance the caterpillar dance, hatching from an egg, getting bigger and bigger, spinning a cocoon then emerging as a beautiful butterfly and fluttering away.
5. Offer strips of paper to make zig-zag books of the caterpillar sequence.

And another idea . . .

* Make butterfly paintings.
* Sing caterpillar songs & rhymes.
* Make some 'life cycle of a butterfly' sequencing cards.
* Keep caterpillars and watch them turn into butterflies.

Links with the Early Learning Goals

MD count reliably up to 10 everyday objects;
recognise numerals 1-9;
use everyday words to describe position;
use developing mathematical ideas and methods to solve practical problems.

Ten Sleepy Sheep

Counting back from 10

Ten lambs are looking for places to sleep. Each one finds somewhere to sleep and in each different place there are opportunities to look for detail in the pictures. Count back from ten and on again as you read and remember the story.

What you need:
☆ the book
☆ ten toy sheep (or cardboard cutouts)
☆ number cards (for older children)

Some key vocabulary

one	eight	count
two	nine	many
three	ten	next
four	and their	last
five	numbers	left
six	sheep	more
seven	lamb	less

Small groups (ideally two or three children) are best for this story. The pictures are gentle and night related, so the detail needs careful looking. There are lots of **counting opportunities in the background** of each picture, so don't miss these additional opportunities.

What you do:

1. Set the sheep in a line and add number cards if you feel the children are ready for them. Put them where you (or the children) can remove one at a time as the story proceeds, starting at 10.
2. Read the story right through first, before using the sheep for counting. Emphasise the rhyme and rhythm as you read or tell the story.
3. Now read the story again, removing one sheep as you read each page, and pausing to count how many are left. Encourage the children to hold up the right number of fingers as you tell the story. This way, they will hear, see and feel the counting, using their senses to help their memory.
4. Use the number cards if the children are ready.
5. If the children are ready for more, or at another time, go through the book counting the bees, stars, swans, ducklings and other creatures in the story.
6. Leave the story and the sheep out with a tray of sand, fake grass or real turf so children can play the story again in free choice time. Offer sticky labels to stick numbers on the sheep.

And another idea . . .

* Talk about day and night and passing time.
* Use other small world animals and people to tell stories that encourage counting on and back from 0 to 10.

Links with the Early Learning Goals

MD say and use number names in order in familiar contexts;
count reliably up to 10 everyday objects;
recognise numerals 1-9;
find one more or one less than a number from 1-10.

Rosie's Walk

'On and back again'

Counting is an 'on and back' process. Rosie's Walk is an old favourite, with masses of mathematical opportunities. Sequence, storying and mathematical vocabulary are all supported and extended, and the pictures have a perfect amount of detail for prediction and recall.

What you need:
- ☆ the book
- ☆ a model duck and a model fox (or card figures with stands)
- ☆ a selection of boxes, tubes etc. for the journey

Some key vocabulary

across	chase
around	follow
over	behind
past	near
through	in
under	on

Rosie's walk is **a circular story**, as Rosie goes for a walk, totally unaware that the fox is just behind her! Children love the anticipation of each page, as they predict what will happen next.

What you do:

1. Start with just Rosie and the fox. Put them where the children can see them as you read the story. Read the book right through without stopping the first time. Then read again, pausing on each page to allow the children to predict what will happen to the fox on the next page. Spot the detail in the picture, the frogs, mice, nests and other animals in the illustrations.
2. Now talk about the way Rosie went round the farmyard. Use mathematical vocabulary such as under, through, behind, on etc.
3. Use your collection of boxes etc. to make Rosie's walk. Take her along the walk and use the position words to describe what she is doing - 'Through the tube, over the box, in the bag, behind the carton etc.'
4. Encourage the children to make new walks for Rosie or the fox (or for Rosie to follow the fox!). Use opened boxes, tubes, flat card for bridges, tubes, rolled card, even some straw or hay from a pet shop. You could make a pond in a plant saucer, and a chicken coop for Rosie to come home to.
5. Reconstruct Rosie's walk, or another walk in the garden of your setting and see if children can follow instructions from you or each other.

And another idea . . .

* Talk about, draw and recon-struct the way children get to school.
* Have an obstacle race with blankets, tunnels, steps etc.

Links with the Early Learning Goals for Maths

MD use everyday words to describe position;
use mathematical ideas & methods to solve practical problems.

Nine Ducks, Nine
Counting back

Nine little ducks are being followed by a fox. Watch them as, one at a time, they leave the group for safer places. Use the story for some practice at counting back, looking for detail and using positional words. You could also practice ordinal numbers, and the difficult concept of 'one less'.

What you need:
☆ the book
☆ nine plastic ducks
☆ number cards to nine

Some key vocabulary

numbers 1-9	left
rhyming words	up/down
gate/eight	ordinal numbers
six/tricks	
four/shore	
three/tree	
less/more	

This is a **rhyming book** and should be read right though before you embark on any maths.

What you do:

1. Read the story through, making the most of the rhymes and vocabulary.
2. Read the story again, stopping to count the ducks on each page. Read the speech bubbles. Use 'more' and 'less', 'more' and 'fewer' as you talk about and count the ducks.
3. Now use the ducks to explore counting back, 'one more', 'one less'.
4. Work with the children to use ordinal numbers as they line up the ducks in a row - first, second, third etc.
5. Ask nine children to stand in a line and play an ordinals game: Try some questions like this:

   'What colour is the second child's hair?'
   'Which child is wearing a yellow jumper?'
   'Go and touch the fourth child in the line.'
   'Stand behind the ninth child.'

6. Give each of the children a number card and practice 'One less than nine is eight; one less than eight is seven' etc. Get the children to sit down as you count back.

And another idea . . .

* Float nine numbered ducks in the water tray and try to catch them in number order with nets.
* Play out the story with bricks or recycled materials.

Links with the Early Learning Goals for Maths

MD recognise numerals 1-9;
count reliably up to 10
everyday objects;
say and use number names in
order.

The Bad Tempered Ladybird

Language of sequence

This story about a ladybird with a bad temper is another favourite. The illustrations give lots of opportunities to discuss sequence and order, before and after, and the story layout encourages a sense of time.

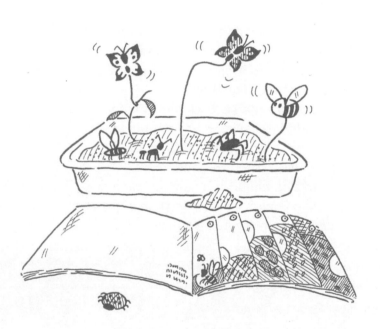

What you need:
☆ the story
☆ a collection of plastic insects and animals
☆ a clock face

Some key vocabulary

numbers to 12	bigger
o'clock	smaller
before	size
after	shape
next	day
big	night
small	

What you do:

1. Read the story right through to start with.
2. Next, use the book to track the ladybird's journey through the day, using the clock if the children are ready for it.
3. Draw the children's attention to the series of animals and insects the ladybird meets. Encourage use of mathematical language - first, second etc. and big, bigger, biggest.
4. Using insects and animals reconstruct the story or if you haven't got the right creatures, make up a new adventure for the ladybird.
5. You could also:
   - ☆ talk about the sequence of the day, from getting up to going to bed;
   - ☆ talk about the order of doing things. Make some simple card sequences, or take digital photos of simple events such as getting dressed, making a sandwich, cleaning your teeth, making a simple recipe, going swimming. Use these to discuss the importance of doing things in the right order. Try them in the wrong order and see what happens!

And another idea . . .

* Put plastic creatures in the sand or some compost to replay sequencing stories.
* Use a drawing or paint program on your computer to recreate the story. Each child could dictate a line or two of text for their picture and then print copies to make a class book. Or you could read the story on screen.

(see The Little Book of ICT for more help and ideas)

Links with the Early Learning Goals for Maths

MD   use language such as greater, smaller, heavier or lighter to compare quantities,

Ten Little Rubber Ducks

Ordinal numbers

A news item about a shipment of 29,000 rubber bath toys falling overboard inspired this story of ten ducks set afloat as they travelled the sea in a container ship. Follow their adventures and practice ordinal numbers as you go.

What you need:

☆ the book
☆ 10 plastic bath ducks or
    10 cards with a duck on each
☆ you could write a number on
    each duck with a permanent
    marker

Some key vocabulary

first, second etc.	east, west
drift	up
water	down
ocean	this way
cargo ship	that way
north, south	day/night

What you do:

1. As always, read the book right through first, enjoying the illustrations and the flow of the story, including the squeaker on the last page!

2. As you read the story again, use the toy ducks to emphasise the ordinal numbers (first, second, third etc.).

3. Pause as you come to the direction words, to check and confirm understanding. Children may need help with the compass points, and you could follow this up with a discussion of weather vanes, wind socks etc.

4. As you continue your re-reading, talk about the different animals each toy duck meets.

5. Help the children to make some simple headbands with yellow 'duck bills' and play out the order of the story with ten children. Extra children could be the captain of the boat, the factory workers, 'real' ducklings and the mother duck in the playing of the story.

6. Make headbands for each of the animals in the story, and you could invite another group to come and see a performance. If you work in a reception class, you could make this story into a mathematical assembly for Key Stage 1 or even the whole school.

And another idea . . .

* Float ten numbered ducks in a water tray and try to catch them in order with aquarium nets.

Links with the Early Learning Goals for Maths

MD   use everyday words to describe position;
count reliably up to 10 every day objects;
recognise numerals 1-9.

Kipper's Toybox

Maths with toys

Kipper is a favourite with all children. In this story he keeps counting the toys in his toy box, but keeps getting a different number! Use this endearing book to enjoy counting together and guessing what happens in the end.

What you need:
☆ the book
☆ an empty cardboard box
☆ six different toys (they can be different from the story)
☆ a Kipper toy, Kipper badge or headband, and 2 mice!

Some key vocabulary

box	again	day
more	empty	
less	full	
missing	in	
count	out	
check	night	

Collect some toys for Kipper's box before you start. Make a badge or headband for Kipper or use a puppet or soft character toy.
<u>You can make simple mice from a circle of card:</u>
Cut a slit from the edge of the circle to the middle and roll the card into a cone. Stick or staple it, add some whiskers, paper ears and a tail, draw some eyes and make a pink nose.

What you do:

1. Read the story right through. Just indicate the toys or their noses as you count in the story.
2. Talk about what happened in the story and how the counting went wrong for Kipper.
3. You could pause here to make some mice with the children. Make them small enough to fit on their finger and you can use them for counting and for rhymes and songs.
4. Show the children the box of toys and let a volunteer count them out onto the floor or table.
5. Now you can play out the story again, with one child as Kipper, others taking a toy each, and a group to be mice and mouse babies.
6. Use the toys for free counting practice, to play out the story or to make up a new one.

And another idea . . .

* Find a copy of the traditional tale of The Seven Sillies, oir Joyce Dunbar's modern version about seven animals who get confused with counting!

Links with the Early Learning Goals for Maths

MD say and use number names in order in familiar contexts; count reliably up to 10 every day objects;
use language such as more, less, to compare 2 numbers;
use developing mathematical ideas and methods to solve practical problems.

The Tiger who Came to Tea

Number One-to-one matching

A little girl is getting ready for teatime when a tiger knocks on the door to invite himself to tea. Teatime stories give lots of opportunities for one-to-one matching as well as sequencing.

What you need:

☆ the story
☆ a tea set; this could be a child's set, a doll's tea set, a picnic set or normal sized
☆ a tablecloth or fabric square

Some key vocabulary

tiger	teapot	beginning
teatime	first	end
kitchen	next	
cup	happened	
saucer	problem	
plate	solve	

NB don't forget to ask 'What if?' and 'What would you do?' questions as you work on sequences, encouraging children to solve problems.

What you do:

1. Tell the story first, then play it out, with children taking the part of the girl and the tiger. Older children could play out the action in pairs as you read the story.
2. Using a teaset, talk with the children about setting a table. Start with a table for two, spreading a cloth and setting matching cups, saucers, plates and cutlery for each person.
3. Repeat the activity for three, four and five people, using such language as 'One for you, and one for you, and one for you - that makes three' etc.
4. Use a washing line to help you talk about the sequences of getting ready for a tea party. There are lots of short sequences you could try:
   Sequencing the process of activities and tasks:
      making a cup of tea
      making cakes or sandwiches
   Sequencing time:
      making and sending invitations (including RSVPs).
5. Read some more teatime stories such as 'The Lighthouse Keeper's Tea', 'Angelina's Teaparty', 'Miss Spider's Tea Party' (a counting story), 'Tea for Ten', 'Tea in the Sugar Bowl', or even the teaparty in 'Alice in Wonderland'.

And another idea . .

* Collect different sizes, patterns, shapes of teasets. Include plastic, china and metal too. Charity shops are a great source of patterned and unusually shaped china oddments, so the interest could extend to a topic on pattern, colour and shape as well as size.

Links with the Early Learning Goals for Maths

MD   use developing mathematical ideas and methods to solve practical problems; 1-1 correspondence.

The Bear Hunt

Sequence and position

A classic for telling, acting, playing out with sounds and actions. This story also helps with the discussion and use of language of position. Using small world figures helps the story along and gives children a chance to replay it, again and again and with variations, on their own.

What you need:

☆ the story
☆ small world figures and a bear to represent the characters
☆ a large piece of paper (the back of a roll of wallpaper would be ideal)
☆ paints, crayons or felt pens

Some key vocabulary

family	in
journey	out
first	back
over	cave
under	chase
through	catch

The Little Book of Maths from Stories

What you do:

1. Prepare the activity in advance. A long sheet of paper conveys a journey well. Decide whether you will use paint, crayons or big felt pens and have these ready. Make sure the group is small enough for everyone to see and to get involved. If you are working with a big group, you could pin the paper on a wall and work with cut out figures stuck on with Blutack, so they can travel through the story.

2. This is such a well known and familiar story for many children that you may not need to read it before starting the activity.

3. Begin to tell the story, using the character figures or cutouts. As you get to each place in the story, stop to draw the river, the mud, the forest etc. Talk about the best way to depict the 'swishy, swashy grass', or the 'icky, sticky mud'. Use the children's ideas and encourage them to make their own picture of the sequence of events.

4. Leave the pictorial story where children can replay it again, either on a wall or in a quiet space on the floor.

5. Turn the story into a movement sequence in a big space indoors or in the garden, where the children can use their whole bodies to tell the adventure. Then add some musical instruments and turn it into a dance sequence.

And another idea . . .

* Make a 3D map in an empty water tray or builder's tray. Use small world people and creatures to make the Bear Hunt and other sequences. Add some pictorial sequence cards.

Links with the Early Learning Goals for Maths

MD use everyday words to describe position;
use developing mathematical ideas and methods to solve practical problems.

Oi! Get Off Our Train

Addition (one more)

John Burnigham's story takes a boy, a dog and a train. Is it a dream or is it real? The story has a contemporary twist with its ecological theme, but there are lots of mathematical opportunities too as more and more animals get on the train.

What you need:
- ☆ the story
- ☆ some small world animals
- ☆ a toy train

Some key vocabulary

train	one less
ride	how many
journey	add
next	take away
together	each
one more	

This story can be used for many different mathematical conversations. The initial one is **'one more'** which can be extended to **'one less'**.

What you do:

1. Tell the story through without stopping.
2. Now look at the pictures. Ask some questions about numbers and counting, such as:

   'How many animals are on the train now?'

   'Who came next?' 'Who came before ....?'

   'How many legs?'

   'How many ears?'

   'How many wings?'

   'One more animal, how many on the train now?'

   'How many kites? How many creatures? Is that one each? If one more animal came with a kite, how many kites would there be? How many creatures?'

   'If there was one animal in each carriage, how long would the train need to be?'

3. Make a train from chairs, cardboard boxes or even cushions. Make a driver's hat and some animal masks or headbands and play the story again.

And another idea . . .

* Make toy trains from recycled materials and cartons. Join the carriages with string and fill the carriages with animals and people. Use the train for 'adult supported' counting, addition and subtraction games as the animals get on and off.

Links with the Early Learning Goals for Maths

MD find one more or one less than a number from 1-10;
begin to relate addition to combining two groups of objects, and subtraction to taking away.

Mrs Armitage on Wheels

More/less

Mrs Armitage adds more and more things to her bike till the inevitable disaster happens! Children love this story and so many follow up activities can be planned - it's sure to become a favourite in your setting.

What you need:

☆ the story
☆ a picture of a bike (cut one from a catalogue or advert and mount on card)
☆ small cards, pens
☆ a washing line and pegs

Some key vocabulary

bike	behind
ride	back/front
next	different
after	idea
many	last
on/under	

Involve the children in this story as they make the cards for the washing line. **You need to prepare the activity beforehand,** and might like to collect the real objects, but some of the things Mrs Armitage adds to her bike are unusual and difficult to get hold of!

What you do:

1. Read the story first, giving the children plenty of time to look at the detail of the pictures.
2. Make sure the children have easy access to the cards and pens, so they can be ready to draw pictures as you all need them.
3. Start your washing line sequence with a picture of the bike.
4. Begin to read the story again, looking at each page and what Mrs Armitage adds next.
5. Ask for a volunteer to draw the picture of each addition on a card, and help the child to peg it to the sequence on the line.
6. Continue to tell the story, adding pictures as Mrs Armitage 'improves' her bike.
7. When you have completed the story, you could add numbers to the objects or use ordinals to name them 'first, second, third...' etc.
8. Use the cards for independent or adult supported maths activities, including 'one more' and sequencing.

And another idea . . .

* Bring one of the bikes in and try making accessories to make it more fun to ride outside. Try giving the children a challenge of making a particular accessory or finding a way to fix things in different places on the bike.
* Go on a 'wheel counting walk' in your setting or community. Count wheels, take photos, make a book.

Links with Early Learning Goals for Maths

MD   use developing mathematical ideas and
methods to solve practical problems;
say and use number names in order in
familiar contexts;
use everyday words to describe position.

The Little Book of Maths from Stories

Handa's Surprise
One less

Calculating

Fruit and food are favourites for maths activities. Use this delightful book to explore the difficult concept of 'one less', as well as exploring the animals, the sequences and even the tastes of the range of fruit in the story.

What you need:
- ☆ the story
- ☆ a flat basket. If you put a square of fabric inside, the fruit won't roll about so much!
- ☆ fruit (plastic or real) to match the story
- ☆ card and pens
- ☆ a scarf or long piece of thin fabric. *Twist this round until you can make a ring to rest on a child's head. The ring will help them balance the basket.*

Some key vocabulary

seven	pineapple	last
six	avocado	full
five	pear	empty
four	passion	big/small
three	fruit	
two	tangerine	
one	basket	
banana	one more	
guava	one less	
orange	first	
mango	next	

Practice in making the fabric ring will not be wasted! Some children may already know how to balance something on their head, others will need the extra support it gives.

What you do:

1. Read the book (if it is a very familiar story, you may just need to get the children to recall the story line).
2. Help the children to make some simple animal headbands or masks, using the book to help with features, patterns, ears etc.
3. Look together at the fruit and the basket. Talk about the different fruit, naming and handling each one. If you use real fruit, talk about the texture and smell of each one.
4. Count the seven fruits into the basket and decide between you who will be each animal and who will be Handa.
5. Count the fruit into the basket, and let Handa put it on her head. Plastic fruit make the basket easier to balance, but real fruit make it much more exciting!
6. Make sure the animals are ready, and choose someone to be Akeyo at the end.
7. Read the story slowly so each animal can gently take the correct fruit from the basket as Handa passes. Handa needs to walk smoothly and slowly!
8. As you tell the story, count down from seven to none as the fruit is taken by the animals.
9. The goat could bring the tangerines to refill the basket for Ayeko's surprise.

And another idea . . .

*   Try eating raisins or grapes one at a time for great 'one less' practice!

Links with Early Learning Goals for Maths

MD count reliably up to 10 everyday objects;
use language such as more, less, to compare 2 numbers;
in practical activities and discussion begin to use the vocabulary involved in addition and subtraction.

Bear in a Square

All sorts of shapes

This is a board book, tough enough for continued handling, and very good for introducing shapes, specially the more unusual ones. Use it as a starting point for shape recognition, a shape theme or a maths topic.

What you need:

☆ the book
☆ card, plastic or wooden shapes
   (check the back of the book to
   make sure you have them all)
☆ sticky or bright coloured
   paper

Some key vocabulary

square	zigzag	curved
circle	star	straight
heart	oval	
rectangle	moon	
diamond	edge	
triangle	corner	

The Little Book of Maths from Stories

Many board books are useful for maths work with groups of older children. **Keep your eyes open for simple books on colours, shapes, animals, body parts, counting etc.**

What you do:

1. Read the book once, emphasising the rhythm and rhymes. This will help children to predict and sequence the story as you read it again.

2. This book is also a counting book - so don't miss the opportunity to count each shape. Revisit each page, spotting the shapes on each page, looking at the different sizes and counting how many. Use the 'one more' language as you go.

3. Now use your collection of shapes to discuss the differences in edges, corners, curved and straight edges in each shape.

4. Try some different ways of sorting the shapes:
   shapes with corners/no corners;
   shapes with curved edges/straight edges;
   shapes with two edges/three edges/four edges/more edges.

5. Work with the children to draw round some of the shapes and cut them out. Arrange the shapes in pictures or patterns, stick them down if you want to, or use and re-use them.

And another idea . . .

* Use stamps, sponge shapes, or potatoes to make shapes for printing or stamping in patterns or pictures. Older children will enjoy making repeating patterns with several shapes.

Links with the Early Learning Goals for Maths

MD   use language such as circle, or bigger to describe the shape and size of solids and flat shapes;
talk about, recognise and recreate simple patterns.

Where's My Teddy?

Discussing size

One of the many stories about the Bear and Eddie, each with a teddy. As well as a very good and very funny story, it gives opportunities for a discussion of relative size, which may even get adults confused!

What you need:

☆ the story
☆ as many different sizes of teddies as you can collect. Try to get some VERY small bears as well as VERY big ones.
☆ small world character children

Some key vocabulary

size	huge
big	great
small	minute
bigger	tall
smaller	massive
tiny	

This may be a familiar story, but it is important to **read it right through** before using it for maths activities.

What you do:

1. Read the story straight through.
2. Show the children all the bears and help them to sort them in order of size. Talk about the biggest, smallest, middle sized. Look at the small world children.
3. Now try some discussion of relative size. Take the biggest teddy and put it next to a small world child. Ask the children to describe the bear's size and the child's size.
4. Now stand up and put the same bear next to you. What size does it look now?
5. Take one of the very small bears. Put it next to the small world child. How does it look? Now put it next to the biggest bear. How does it look? Now next to a child. How does it look? Encourage use of descriptive words such as huge, tiny, massive. Is the bear still the same size?
6. Some children will find this discussion very difficult! How can something be big AND small, gigantic AND minute? Give the children plenty of time and space to talk about these concepts and make their own suggestions. Ask 'What do <u>you</u> think? Don't rush to explain the idea of relative size.

Links with Early Learning Goals for Maths

MD use language such as circle, or bigger to describe the shape and size of solids and flat shapes;
use language such as greater, smaller, heavier or lighter to compare quantities.

And another idea . . .

* Leave the bears and small world characters in a basket for further discussion and experiment as children check their growing understanding of relative size.
* Read My Friend Bear, which continues the friendship and the concept of size and character.

Follow My Leader

Position

A rhythmical story of a boy, his animal friends and a tiger. This story is great to dramatise and gives you opportunities for discussing and remembering position as the line of animals gets longer, then shorter.

What you need:
- ☆ the book
- ☆ animals, or animal masks for the animals in the story
- ☆ a small drum or tambourine

Some key vocabulary

animal	up	behind
names	down	
next	over	
first	under	
last	round	
positions	through	

The Little Book of Maths from Stories

Read the story right through, **emphasising the rhythm and rhyme.**
Don't stop or the children will lose the sense of the story.

What you do:

1. Now you could spend some time together making simple animal masks or headbands, or collecting together (or making) small world animals to use in playing out the story.

2. Re-read the story (younger children will need to refresh their memory of the order). Get the children to sit in the right order, either wearing headbands/masks, or holding an animal each.

3. Now tell each page slowly, talking about who came next and adding them to the line of animals. Continue till the animals are all present and the tiger appears (a tambourine or drum might be useful at this point!).

4. Pause and remind the children that the animals now go away one at a time, and read the second half of the story till the boy and his dog get back to their house and the tiger marches off into the distance.

5. Use small world animals or children for a discussion about position - who came first, next, fifth, last?

And another idea . . .

* As the children get used to it, try playing the story faster with a tambourine to keep the rhythm. Go outside or in a big space for this!
* Tape the story for children to read or act out.

Links with the Early Learning Goals for Maths

MD in practical activities and discussion begin to use the vocabulary involved in addition & subtraction; use language such as more, less, to compare 2 numbers; use everyday words to describe position.

Pants

Discussing pattern

Children will delight in this slightly 'naughty' rhyming book about underwear.
The book is memorable for its pictures and its words, and provides a good
starting point for a topic or discussion on pattern and colour as well as
matching pants to people!

What you need:

☆ a collection of (clean!) pants
of different sorts, colours,
patterns and types

☆ a washing line and pegs

Some key vocabulary

stripes	small	leg
spots	bigger	stretch
squares	smaller	
flowers	tiny	
pattern	short	
big	long	

This is a good book to start a topic on **shape and colour,** or to help children explore either of these concepts. If you are using a washing line, set this up before you read the book.

What you do:

1. Read to book right through, just showing the pictures as you go. Keep the rhythm of the book and emphasise the rhymes. This will help the children to remember the order of the pages.

2. Now read the story again pausing on each page to talk about the pictures, the patterns and the rhymes. Children will love the rather risky subject matter!

3. Concentrate on the mathematical aspect you have chosen and remember to use mathematical vocabulary when discussing the illustrations.

4. Now ask a child volunteer to choose a pair of pants from your collection. Help them to peg the pants on the line and tell you about them - they may need prompts to include shape, size, colour and pattern as well as identifying the possible wearer.

5. Continue to select and hang different pairs of pants on your line, discussing each pair.

6. Why not cut out some paper outlines of pants and decorate them with different patterns, styles and colours. Use collage bits of lace etc. to decorate the pants.

And another idea . . .

* Try some grouping of the pants - boys/girls; adult/child; all plain/all patterned; with/without writing etc.

* You could use a collection of socks, teeshirts, gloves etc. to sort and discuss.

Links with the Early Learning Goals for Maths

MD   talk about, recognise and recreate simple patterns;

Blue Balloon
Transformation

Balloons are one of the best resources for exploring transformation - this book needs real examples. The story can be used to start a real discussion of change, which may lead you across the curriculum into every area.

What you need:
- ☆ the book
- ☆ some balloons and a balloon pump
- ☆ some 3D shapes

Some key vocabulary

big	up	stretch
bigger	down	long
small	shape	
smaller	changed	
round	here	
square	there	

This book is all about changes, so you may want to use it as the start of an **investigation** or start by looking at and talking about things that change. You could look at ice, water, shadows, puddles, corn flour, cooking, dissolving etc.

What you do:

1. Read the book right through, taking some time to demonstrate the folding pages and the changes that happen.
2. Now try blowing up some balloons together, looking at how the balloon changes as you fill it with air.
3. Pass the balloons around and feel them in your hands. Toss them in the air and see how they fall. Talk about the differences between the balloons you have and the one in the story which went on up and up.
4. Make sure each child has an inflated balloon as you read the story again, stopping on each page to discuss the balloon and what happens - use mathematical language to discuss shape, size, direction etc. Have fun making noises, and trying to stick the balloons on the wall or even the ceiling.
5. Some of the children may have had helium filled balloons at fairs and parties. Talk about these and the danger of letting go of the string!

And another idea . . .

* Make up some stories about journeys on the end of a balloon string.
* Get the Little Book of Investigations. It has more ideas about investigating changes like melting, freezing, dissolving.
* Make a transformations dance or movement story.

Links with the Learning Goals for Maths

MD   use everyday words to describe position; use language such as circle, or bigger to describe the shape and size of solids; use developing mathematical ideas and methods to solve practical problems.

Brown Bear

Colour

There are many books which focus on colour. This popular book has been a
favourite for years and is an excellent start to a project or theme of
colours.

What you need:
- ☆ the book
- ☆ small world animals to match
  the book (it would be fun to
  paint them the same colours
  as in the book). Or make a
  headband of each animal.

Some key vocabulary
animal names
colours
next
after
then

What you do:

1. Read the book right through, then talk with the children about the book, the rhymes and rhythm and the different animals.
2. Now you could work with the children either to find and paint animals for the story or make some simple headbands with animal pictures on (each in the right colour for the book).
3. Give each child an animal or a headband and read the book again, encouraging the children to join in with the rhyme, and standing up or holding up the correct animal as the story proceeds.
4. Try making up some additional animals of different colours, such as a pink cow, an orange snake, a grey donkey.
   You could try some more exotic shades with older children, such as a periwinkle toad, a ruby snail, a turquoise worm, a mauve butterfly, a heliotrope bat etc.
5. Add some pages to the book and tell the story again. Remember to always finish with the children and the monkey!

And another idea . . .

* Get some paint shade cards from a DIY store and talk about the names of paint colours.
* Do colour mixing with paint, felt pen, jelly, pastels, dough.
* Make colour collections in baskets, boxes, bags or on washing lines.
* Buy some colour tester pots and redecorate your role play area.

Links with the Early Learning Goals for Maths

MD use mathematical language to describe colour;
use developing mathematical ideas to solve problems.

Jim and the Beanstalk

Measuring

Size, shape and distance are all contained in Raymond Briggs' retelling of Jack and the beanstalk. Take your measuring discussions into technology and creativity as well as maths and language.

What you need:

☆ the book
☆ tape measures and lengths of string
☆ some foil covered chocolate coins
☆ a big piece of paper

Some key vocabulary

big	tiny	down
huge	short	near
massive	little	far
gigantic	teeny	measure
colossal	short	pay
small	up	fit

Collect the things you need and read the story first - **it's different from the traditional one in many ways!**

What you do:

1. Read the story to the children.
2. Talk about the way the story differs from the traditional Jack and the Beanstalk.
3. Now go through the book, talking with the children about the measuring in the story. Use mathematical language and encourage the children to use it too.
4. Talk with the children about the way they could make a pair of glasses, false teeth or a wig for a giant. What could they use? What would be the problems and difficulties?
5. Look at the pages where Jack is measuring the giant, and look together at some tape measures. Older children could find the beginning and see how far they can count the numbers.
6. Use the tape measures (or some pieces of paper, string or ribbon) to experiment with measuring. The children could measure each other's heads, arms, feet, noses. Help them to understand the importance of staring at the right end of the measuring tape and reading the number carefully. Compare measurements of different children, either in numbers or in the length of the string/ribbon needed.

And another idea . . .

* Grow beans and measure them every day.
* Use strings and tapes in free play to measure things indoors and outside.

Links with the Goals for Maths

MD   use language such as circle or bigger to describe the shape and size of solids and flat shapes;
use everyday words to describe position;
use developing mathematical ideas & methods to solve practical problems.

The Little Book of Maths from Stories

What's the Time Mr Wolf?

Shape, Space Measures

Time

The old playground rhyme is used in Colin Hawkins' book about Mr Wolf's day. Children (and some adults) find the passing of time a difficult concept to grasp, so let Mr Wolf help you to find out about clocks and time.

What you need:

☆ the book
☆ a card or plastic clock face with moving hands and/or a digital clock with clear numbers
☆ a real 'alarm type' clock

Some key vocabulary

o'clock	break-	watch
time	fast time	alarm
day	lunchtime	
morning	teatime	
afternoon	bedtime	
evening	clock	

What you do:

1. Read the book all the way through, making the most of the suspense and surprise elements.
   Use a scary voice for Mr Wolf and have fun! The way you tell the story will be a key feature in its success.

2. Look at the book again, spotting the different clocks in the pictures. Get the children to help you to make your clock face the same as the one in each picture.

3. Play the game 'What's the Time Mr Wolf?'.
   * One player stands with their back to the rest of the children.
   * The children take a step towards the wolf chanting 'What's the time Mr (or Mrs) Wolf?'
   * The 'Wolf' replies 'One o'clock' (or any time they choose).
   * The children continue to ask the question, getting nearer to the wolf each time.
   * Eventually the 'wolf' answers 'DINNER TIME!' Then s/he turns round and chases the other children. The first player to get caught is the wolf next.

4. Collect different sorts of clocks and look at each one. Don't forget to include watches and digital clocks. Make a display of 'time telling'.

And another idea . . .

* Go on a 'clock spotting' walk round your setting or your community.
* Make a book of the day with clock faces showing different times and activities. Make it on the computer, using clip art clocks and watches to illustrate your own Mr Wolf book.

Links with the Early Learning Goals for Maths

MD   say and use number names in order in the context of time;
     recognise numerals 1-12.

The Great Pet Sale

Money

A boy has a purse full of money to spend. How can he get the best value at the Pet Sale, despite the pestering pet rat? Delightful illustrations and pages that change make this story a winner as well as a good place to discuss money and prices.

What you need:
☆ the book
☆ a purse and change totalling £1
☆ small world animals to match the ones in the book (optional) Or you could use animal masks, badges or puppets

Some key vocabulary

sale	enough
cheap	too much
reduced	left over
money	choose
sold	
pay	

Read the book yourself so you know what happens and how to make sure you tell this story in a way that your children can understand. **Younger children may find the amounts of money in the story beyond their experience and understanding** - don't worry about this, it's a great story for all ages, and the important concept is about paying!

What you do:

1. As usual, it's best to read the story straight through first, avoiding pauses for comment. If children get used to this way of reading books, they will be much more involved in what happens next and the flow of the story from page to page.
2. Now talk about the pet sale, what a sale is and why the children think the different animals are in the Pet Sale.
3. Make some badges or headbands, or find some animals or puppets so you can retell the story. Then, with a child to be the boy in the story, read the book again with actions, money and joining in with the words.
4. A small group of older children may be ready to talk about the money, taking the right amount from the purse to match the amount on each page. This is quite a difficult activity, so don't embark on it if you think it is beyond them. Just enjoy the story and the activity of counting out and paying.

And another idea . . .

* Have your own pet shop or pet sale, using soft toy animals. Get the children to bring their own from home.
* Read the book 'Dogger' by Shirley Hughes, about a very special toy dog that got lost and put in a sale by mistake.
* Add some purses and money to your role play areas. Start with 1p and 2p coins. Real money is much more fun than plastic.

Links with the Early Learning Goals for Maths

MD   count reliably up to 10 everyday objects; and begin to understand and use coins.

Mr Archimedes

Capacity

Mr Archimedes can't understand how the water from his bath gets all over the floor! He shares his bath with some animals friends and tries to find out what happens when they all get in. Water play on a large scale!

What you need:
☆ the book
☆ a container of water (preferably transparent)
☆ some small world people and plastic animals (the ones in the story are a bit unusual!)

Some key vocabulary

sale	enough
cheap	too much
reduced	left over
money	choose
sold	
pay	

You may not have a toy goat, wombat and kangaroo, so find some other animals! Make sure they are heavy enough to displace some water, and make sure the 'bath' is not too big or the results of your experiment will be difficult to see.

You will also need a plastic sheet, a ruler or stick and a marker pen.

What you do:

1. Read the story right through, enjoying the overflowing bath and the voices of the animals.
2. Now talk with the children about what happened and see if they have worked out why the bath overflowed.
3. Fill your container with water and experiment with the animals etc. seeing if you can replicate the story. You may just want to use a stick to measure the difference as the water rises, marking it with a permanent pen so you can see the difference.
4. Read the story again, encouraging the children to join in the voices, specially the shouting and EUREKA!
5. Continue the experiments (outside if possible) with containers of different sizes, plain or coloured water and any objects the children find. Stones and real bricks work well, sand has a more gradual effect, so they can get the water exactly to the top of the container by adding a little at a time.

And another idea . . .

* Make some simple rain gauges from plastic pop bottles. Cut across below the shoulders of the bottle and invert the top to make a funnel.
* Construct a waterway from guttering and drainpipes to float boats and other things up and down.
* Offer very small scoops, spoons, funnels, droppers and containers to fill and empty.

Links with the Early Learning Goals for Maths

MD   use everyday words to describe position; use developing mathematical ideas and methods to solve practical problems.

Don't Forget the Bacon
Remembering

Topics

A classic story about a boy who forgets what his mother has asked him to buy. Its repeated refrain encourages joining in and the listening skills needed to avoid getting muddled are substantial. Counting, money, memory, listening, writing, are all included.

What you need:
- ☆ the book
- ☆ a basket
- ☆ paper and pen for list making
- ☆ pictures or objects (the ones on the list)

Some key vocabulary

list	mistake
buy	right
remember	wrong
order	next
forget	first
muddle	last

You may need to do some preparation for this story. **The objects are easy to make** (an egg box, a cake made from 2 round pieces of foam sandwiched with red paint, a bag of plastic pears, a pack of pretend bacon). The memory and rhyming is helped by some concrete visual props.

What you do:

1. Read the story right through, emphasising the rhyme and rhythm.
2. Now talk with the children about what went wrong and why the boy got in such a muddle. Do they ever get in a muddle when they are trying to remember things? Use a few examples to help, like getting the letters in your name in the wrong order, bringing PE kit on the wrong day, calling your teacher 'Mum' by mistake etc. Try to emphasise that making mistakes is OK, the important thing is having a go, trying your best, not getting upset when you make a mistake, and practising (some children, and many adults find this difficult!).
3. Try playing some simple games like 'Simon Says', 'I went to the supermarket and I bought....' or 'Kim's Game'.
4. Get a child volunteer to be the boy (with or without a dog) as you read the story again. Other children could mime the mother, the shopkeepers, the other people.

And another idea . . .

* Offer paper and pens for list making in your writing area.
* Play number memory by saying three or four numbers for a child to repeat back to you.
* Play Chinese whispers with numbers round a circle, so the children see how important it is to listen carefully.
* Practise remembering phone numbers, birthdays and addresses.

Links with the Early Learning Goals for Maths

MD use developing mathematical ideas and methods to solve practical problems.

Mrs Lather's Laundry
Clothes

One in a series of Happy Family has a problem - she is bored with just washing clothes, so she decides to try some other things! This book is a good starter for a project on clothes, pattern or sorting.

What you need:
- ☆ the book
- ☆ a collection of clothes and other washable items
- ☆ washing baskets
- ☆ a washing line and pegs
- ☆ aprons and shower caps

Some key vocabulary

wash	shape
big	material
small	fabric
pair	bubbles
pattern	clothes
size	

Prepare for this activity by collecting some clothing - go for a good range of sizes, shapes, patterns etc. Include some pairs of socks, gloves, baby clothes, even dolls' clothes to ensure plenty of mathematical choices. The story is really just a starter for a whole range of other activities

What you do:

1. Read the story right through, and discuss what happened, trying to model mathematical language wherever possible.
2. Now explore the clothes basket of washing. Talk about the mathematical properties of each - size, shape, colour, pattern etc. Look at the things that come in pairs and try counting in twos.
3. Use your washing line and pegs to peg the clothes up - make a line of baby clothes or paired socks or clothes with legs /buttons/zips, or big clothes - the children will be able to come up with more mathematical sorting ideas!
4. Older children can use the opportunity to count pegs in twos as they hang the items on the line.
5. You could have a real washing day with real water, bubbles and clothes to wash - this is better done outside with waterproof aprons!

And another idea . . .

* Have Mrs Lather's Laundry as a role play focus. Offer clothes, babies, dogs, socks, vests in separate baskets for different experiences.
* Visit a launderette or go on a local walk to spot washing lines in gardens.

Links with the Early Learning Goals for Maths

MD   use language such as circle or bigger to describe the shape and size of solids and flat shapes;
use developing mathematical ideas & methods to solve practical problems.

Alfie's Feet
Shoes

Alfie goes to the shoe shop for a new pair of Wellington boots. However, something is wrong when he starts to puddle jump! Follow the fun and use the story for some follow up work on pairs, on shoes, on rain or on shopping.

What you need:
- ☆ the story
- ☆ some pairs of boots and shoes
- ☆ card for labels
- ☆ pegs for pairing shoes & boots

Some key vocabulary

pair	colour	left
big	shape	muddle
small	pattern	
bigger	laces	
smaller	velcro	
choose	right	

Children will empathise with this story - not being allowed to splash in puddles in your shoes, getting them on the wrong feet, choosing which colour to have - all big decisions and a good way to start looking at **pairs, counting in twos or sorting for size**. Decide which maths aspects you will concentrate on, so you don't get distracted.

What you do:

1. Read the story right through, turning pages slowly so the children can see the pictures, but not stopping for comments at this stage.
2. Revisit the parts of the story the children like best before moving on to the mathematical focus.
3. Now its your turn to choose some of the pages to look at again, selecting those which focus on your chosen theme for the session.
4. Use mathematical language to explore the focus with the children (it might be colour, shape, size, pairing).
5. Explore your collection of shoes and boots (you could put some odd ones in if you are focusing on pairing). Keep your mathematical focus, but listen to suggestions and thoughts the children offer. Keep pairs together with pegs.
6. You could display your shoes and boots in a row for counting sorting or size matching.

And another idea . . .

* Put prices and sizes on the shoes and make a shoe shop.
* Go outside in the wet and do some puddle jumping!
* Borrow/buy a children's foot measure and measure everyone's feet.
* Help the children to draw round their feet for matching and comparing sizes.
* Make footprints in paint, water, sand and compare.

Links with the Early Learning Goals for Maths

MD use language such as greater, smaller, heavier or lighter to compare quantities; count in 2s (level 1)

Bet You Can't

Growing and growing up

Topics

Two children are cleaning up at bedtime. There is the usual argument about who is bigger, stronger, older, with some messy results! This book is great for picture spotting, for counting and for discussing the fact that older MAY not mean bigger, taller or stronger and co-operation is best.

What you need:
☆ the book
☆ a basket of toys
☆ a height measure or a place where you can mark and name children's heights

Some key vocabulary

bigger	stronger
smaller	weaker
older	heavy
younger	light
taller	together
shorter	

The Little Book of Maths from Stories

Inside the cover of this book there is a pictorial list of the contents of the basket. Most of the items are easy to collect, so, given a bit of notice, you could collect the right objects to really replicate the story. This will enable you to do **lots of spotting, matching and sorting** as well as talking about growing stronger.

What you do:

1. Read the story through,
2. Now talk about what happened in the story, revisiting some of the pages as the children recall the events.
3. Tip out your basket and talk about what it contains. Pick an item, turn to one of the pages and see if you can spot it in the picture. Children love this game of close observation, and it helps them learn to discriminate between the shapes of different numbers and letters.
4. Now talk about growing and growing up. Use a height measure or a place on the wall or door frame to mark and measure each child's height. Compare the heights and talk about tallest, oldest, shortest, youngest. Make it clear that tallest or oldest is not best! Ask them to think of the benefits of being smaller or younger (they may need some help or examples such as Stuart Little or Tom Thumb).

And another idea . . .

* Leave the basket and story out for free choice sorting and spotting.
* Measure children's heights again after a month and see who has grown. Repeat this throughout the year, and compare their growth. Be sensitive to the feelings of smaller members of your group!

Links with the Early Learning Goals for Maths

MD   use language such as circle, or bigger to describe the shape and size of solids and flat shapes; use developing mathematical ideas and methods to solve practical problems.

Danny's Birthday
Problem solving

How can Danny find out who sent him his birthday presents? Encourage problem solving techniques in some simple activities inspired by this story.

What you need:
- ☆ the book
- ☆ some parcels wrapped in birthday paper
- ☆ more gift wrapping materials for parcels
- ☆ sticky labels or gift tags

Some key vocabulary

shape	each
size	from
think	birthday
guess	label
parcel	match
different	

This book is a very good **starter for problem solving**. Guess what's in the parcel is a good game, so prepare some mystery parcels beforehand.

What you do:

1. Read the story right through. Then read it again and see how much the children can remember about which present really came from which person.

2. Now look at the mystery parcels. Let the children handle them and see if they can guess what is in them.
   You could have:
   * just some wrapped parcels with no labels;
   * labelled parcels with pictures of the recipient on each (a gift for a baby, a boy, a girl, a grandad, a dog, a policeman, a ballerina etc.);
   * some separate labels which have 'fallen off' so children can try to match the label to the parcel before and after they unwrap each one.

3. Make up another story about mixed up parcels and how the postman could sort them out.

4. Offer some paper and tape for wrapping objects and toys from the room to make mystery parcels for each other. Then have a guess at the contents before opening them.

And another idea . . .

* Put a mystery parcel in the garden before the children arrive and see what happens.
* Turn the role play area into a Post Office and Sorting Office with a postman for deliveries, stamps, posting box and post bags.
* Talk about Post Codes and street numbers and how they help us find our way about. Try your setting's post code in a route finder web site such as Mappy.co.uk to see how Post Codes and house numbers work to help find an address.

Links with the Early Learning Goals for Maths

MD use language such as circle, or bigger to describe the shape and size of solids & flat shapes; use developing mathematical ideas and methods to solve practical problems.

One Bear at Bedtime
Favourite toys

Toys will give you many mathematical opportunities. Use this lovely story about bedtime for counting, but you could also use it for a host of other discussions about favourite toys, times of day, numbers, night time fears and more.

What you need:
- ☆ the book
- ☆ a bear
- ☆ a pair of pyjamas, toothbrush and other bedtime things

Some key vocabulary

numbers	night
to 10	safe
next	
after	
how many	
much	

What you do:

This story stands on its own as a lovely experience, but there is much more to it!

Here are a few ideas for activities to follow a reading of the story:

* Read the story and talk about favourite bedtime toys.
* Find the caterpillars on each page.
* Be each animal in turn as the story is read.
* Bring a favourite toy to the setting for the day (don't forget to send them home again or you will be in trouble at bedtime!). Use the toys for mathematical activities - size, sorting, shape, colour.
* Use the story as a starter for talking about being scared and how it is OK to need a bit of reassurance. Talk about fears and worries openly.
* Use bedtime rituals and activities to explore time passing, and reasons for doing things.
* Make a collection of all the stories you can find with teddies in them - you will be surprised how many there are!
* Discuss health topics such as the importance of enough rest and sleep, cleaning teeth, washing etc.

And another idea . . .

* Make up another story about a favourite toy called 'One Duck at Bathtime,' 'One Dog at Walk Time.'
* Put little number cards in small Zip Lock plastic bags and let the children collect small objects - 6 leaves, 4 paper clips, 8 counters, 7 beads, 4 cubes, 10 pasta shapes etc.

Links with the Early Learning Goals for Maths

MD say and use number names in order in familiar contexts; count reliably up to 10 everyday objects.

A final note from Sally Featherstone

This book was inspired by one of Neil's 'Story telling for Maths' sessions, which I attended in Llandindrod Wells, along with about 200 early years practitioners. Neil is probably the only person I would trust to paint my hands red when I was wearing a new jacket and had not yet presented my afternoon conference session, and that is just what happened!

On that day that I persuaded Neil to work with us on a Little Book, and the Little Book of Maths from Stories is the result of our collaboration. Neil contributed his enormous knowledge of titles and ideas, all I had to do was to link them with the Foundation Stage Guidance and put them in the Little Book format. I have enjoyed the process enormously, and Neil and I both hope you enjoy using the book.

Neil is also writing a longer book, to be called 'Count on Stories' in which he continues to explore the way story telling can help with mathematical learning. We look forward to publishing this book later in 2005.

You can contact Neil for training, Storysacks, and other resources through:
Ruth Bodsworth
National Sales Manager
Storysacks
Tel: 01279 870884
Mobile: 07979 921161

Resources, including Storysacks from:
Corner to learn Ltd, Willow Cottage,
26 Purton Stoke, Swindon, Wilts SN5 4JF
Tel: 01793 421168
Fax: 01793 421168
e-mail: neil@cornertolearn.co.uk
web site: www.storysack.com

If you have found this book useful you might also like ...

**The Little Book of
Cooking From Stories**
LB7
ISBN 1-904187-04-8

**The Little Book of
Maths Songs & Games**
LB12
ISBN 1-904187-32-3

**The Little Book of
Storytelling**
LB19
ISBN 1-904187-65-X

Cooking Up a Story
CUS
ISBN 1-905019-00-9

All available from

Featherstone Education   PO Box 6350
Lutterworth   LE17 6ZA

T:0185 888 1212   F:0185 888 1360

on our web site

www.featherstone.uk.com

and from selected
book suppliers

The Little Books Club

Little Books meet the need for exciting and practical activities which are fun to do, address the Early Learning Goals and can be followed in most settings. As one user put it *"When everything else falls apart I know I can reach for a Little Book and things will be fine!"*

We publish 10 Little Books a year – one every month except for August and December. **Little Books Club members receive each <u>new</u> Little Book on approval** and **at a reduced price** as soon as it's published.

Examine the book at your leisure. Keep it or return it. You decide.

That's all. No strings.   No joining fee.

No agreement to buy a set number of books during the year.

And you can leave at any time.

Little Books Club members receive -

♥   *each new Little Book on approval as soon as it's published*

♥   *a specially reduced price on that book and on any other Little Books they buy*

♥   *a regular, free newsletter dealing with club news and aspects of Early Years curriculum and practice*

♥   *free postage on anything ordered from our catalogue*

♥   *a discount voucher on joining which can be used to buy from our catalogue*

♥   *at least one other special offer every month*

There's always something in Little Books to inspire and help you!

Phone 0185 888 1212 for details